My Bird V

CW01660234

My Bird Watching Journal

My Bird Watching Journal

My Bird Watching Journal

This Book Belongs To:

Publisher: Barry Hutchinson

My Bird Watching Journal

First Edition: June 2022

ISBN 978-1-4716-5270-7

Publisher: Barry Hutchinson

My Bird Watching Journal

Date:	**Time:**	
Season:	**Habitat:**	
Location:		
Weather:	**Temperature:**	
Name of Bird:	**Type of Bird:**	
Type of Tail? ☐ **Short** ☐ **Wide** ☐ **Fluffy** ☐ **Thin** ☐ **Long**	**Shape of Beak?** ☐ **Long & thin** ☐ **Short and pointed** ☐ **Flat and wide** ☐ **Hooked** ☐ **Cone**	**Birds Location?** ☐ **Tree** ☐ **Bush** ☐ **Feeder** ☐ **Fence** ☐ **Ground**
Any colours and markings:		
Bird's actions:		
Notes:		
Sketch/drawing:		

My Bird Watching Journal

Date:	**Time:**	
Season:	**Habitat:**	
Location:		
Weather:	**Temperature:**	
Name of Bird:	**Type of Bird:**	
Type of Tail? ☐ Short ☐ Wide ☐ Fluffy ☐ Thin ☐ Long	**Shape of Beak?** ☐ Long & thin ☐ Short and pointed ☐ Flat and wide ☐ Hooked ☐ Cone	**Birds Location?** ☐ Tree ☐ Bush ☐ Feeder ☐ Fence ☐ Ground
Any colours and markings:		
Bird's actions:		
Notes:		
Sketch/drawing:		

My Bird Watching Journal

<table>
<tr><td>Date:</td><td colspan="2">Time:</td></tr>
<tr><td>Season:</td><td colspan="2">Habitat:</td></tr>
<tr><td colspan="3">Location:</td></tr>
<tr><td>Weather:</td><td colspan="2">Temperature:</td></tr>
<tr><td>Name of Bird:</td><td colspan="2">Type of Bird:</td></tr>
<tr><td>Type of Tail?

☐ Short
☐ Wide
☐ Fluffy
☐ Thin
☐ Long</td><td>Shape of Beak?

☐ Long & thin
☐ Short and pointed
☐ Flat and wide
☐ Hooked
☐ Cone</td><td>Birds Location?

☐ Tree
☐ Bush
☐ Feeder
☐ Fence
☐ Ground</td></tr>
<tr><td colspan="3">Any colours and markings:</td></tr>
<tr><td colspan="3">Bird's actions:</td></tr>
<tr><td colspan="3">Notes:</td></tr>
<tr><td colspan="3">Sketch/drawing:</td></tr>
</table>

My Bird Watching Journal

Date:	**Time:**	
Season:	**Habitat:**	
Location:		
Weather:	**Temperature:**	
Name of Bird:	**Type of Bird:**	
Type of Tail? ☐ Short ☐ Wide ☐ Fluffy ☐ Thin ☐ Long	**Shape of Beak?** ☐ Long & thin ☐ Short and pointed ☐ Flat and wide ☐ Hooked ☐ Cone	**Birds Location?** ☐ Tree ☐ Bush ☐ Feeder ☐ Fence ☐ Ground
Any colours and markings:		
Bird's actions:		
Notes:		
Sketch/drawing:		

My Bird Watching Journal

Date:	Time:	
Season:	Habitat:	
Location:		
Weather:	Temperature:	
Name of Bird:	Type of Bird:	
Type of Tail? ☐ Short ☐ Wide ☐ Fluffy ☐ Thin ☐ Long	Shape of Beak? ☐ Long & thin ☐ Short and pointed ☐ Flat and wide ☐ Hooked ☐ Cone	Birds Location? ☐ Tree ☐ Bush ☐ Feeder ☐ Fence ☐ Ground
Any colours and markings:		
Bird's actions:		
Notes:		
Sketch/drawing:		

My Bird Watching Journal

Date:	**Time:**	
Season:	**Habitat:**	
Location:		
Weather:	**Temperature:**	
Name of Bird:	**Type of Bird:**	
Type of Tail? ☐ Short ☐ Wide ☐ Fluffy ☐ Thin ☐ Long	**Shape of Beak?** ☐ Long & thin ☐ Short and pointed ☐ Flat and wide ☐ Hooked ☐ Cone	**Birds Location?** ☐ Tree ☐ Bush ☐ Feeder ☐ Fence ☐ Ground
Any colours and markings:		
Bird's actions:		
Notes:		
Sketch/drawing:		

My Bird Watching Journal

Date:	Time:	
Season:	Habitat:	
Location:		
Weather:	Temperature:	
Name of Bird:	Type of Bird:	
Type of Tail? ☐ Short ☐ Wide ☐ Fluffy ☐ Thin ☐ Long	Shape of Beak? ☐ Long & thin ☐ Short and pointed ☐ Flat and wide ☐ Hooked ☐ Cone	Birds Location? ☐ Tree ☐ Bush ☐ Feeder ☐ Fence ☐ Ground
Any colours and markings:		
Bird's actions:		
Notes:		
Sketch/drawing:		

My Bird Watching Journal

Date:	**Time:**
Season:	**Habitat:**
Location:	
Weather:	**Temperature:**
Name of Bird:	**Type of Bird:**

Type of Tail?	**Shape of Beak?**	**Birds Location?**
☐ Short	☐ Long & thin	☐ Tree
☐ Wide	☐ Short and pointed	☐ Bush
☐ Fluffy	☐ Flat and wide	☐ Feeder
☐ Thin	☐ Hooked	☐ Fence
☐ Long	☐ Cone	☐ Ground

Any colours and markings:
Bird's actions:
Notes:
Sketch/drawing:

My Bird Watching Journal

Date:	**Time:**	
Season:	**Habitat:**	
Location:		
Weather:	**Temperature:**	
Name of Bird:	**Type of Bird:**	
Type of Tail? ☐ Short ☐ Wide ☐ Fluffy ☐ Thin ☐ Long	**Shape of Beak?** ☐ Long & thin ☐ Short and pointed ☐ Flat and wide ☐ Hooked ☐ Cone	**Birds Location?** ☐ Tree ☐ Bush ☐ Feeder ☐ Fence ☐ Ground
Any colours and markings:		
Bird's actions:		
Notes:		
Sketch/drawing:		

My Bird Watching Journal

Date:	Time:	
Season:	Habitat:	
Location:		
Weather:	Temperature:	
Name of Bird:	Type of Bird:	
Type of Tail? ☐ Short ☐ Wide ☐ Fluffy ☐ Thin ☐ Long	Shape of Beak? ☐ Long & thin ☐ Short and pointed ☐ Flat and wide ☐ Hooked ☐ Cone	Birds Location? ☐ Tree ☐ Bush ☐ Feeder ☐ Fence ☐ Ground
Any colours and markings:		
Bird's actions:		
Notes:		
Sketch/drawing:		

My Bird Watching Journal

Date:	**Time:**	
Season:	**Habitat:**	
Location:		
Weather:	**Temperature:**	
Name of Bird:	**Type of Bird:**	
Type of Tail? ☐ Short ☐ Wide ☐ Fluffy ☐ Thin ☐ Long	**Shape of Beak?** ☐ Long & thin ☐ Short and pointed ☐ Flat and wide ☐ Hooked ☐ Cone	**Birds Location?** ☐ Tree ☐ Bush ☐ Feeder ☐ Fence ☐ Ground
Any colours and markings:		
Bird's actions:		
Notes:		
Sketch/drawing:		

My Bird Watching Journal

Date:	**Time:**	
Season:	**Habitat:**	
Location:		
Weather:	**Temperature:**	
Name of Bird:	**Type of Bird:**	
Type of Tail? ☐ **Short** ☐ **Wide** ☐ **Fluffy** ☐ **Thin** ☐ **Long**	**Shape of Beak?** ☐ **Long & thin** ☐ **Short and pointed** ☐ **Flat and wide** ☐ **Hooked** ☐ **Cone**	**Birds Location?** ☐ **Tree** ☐ **Bush** ☐ **Feeder** ☐ **Fence** ☐ **Ground**
Any colours and markings:		
Bird's actions:		
Notes:		
Sketch/drawing:		

My Bird Watching Journal

Date:	**Time:**	
Season:	**Habitat:**	
Location:		
Weather:	**Temperature:**	
Name of Bird:	**Type of Bird:**	
Type of Tail? ☐ Short ☐ Wide ☐ Fluffy ☐ Thin ☐ Long	**Shape of Beak?** ☐ Long & thin ☐ Short and pointed ☐ Flat and wide ☐ Hooked ☐ Cone	**Birds Location?** ☐ Tree ☐ Bush ☐ Feeder ☐ Fence ☐ Ground
Any colours and markings:		
Bird's actions:		
Notes:		
Sketch/drawing:		

My Bird Watching Journal

<table>
<tr><td>Date:</td><td colspan="2">Time:</td></tr>
<tr><td>Season:</td><td colspan="2">Habitat:</td></tr>
<tr><td colspan="3">Location:</td></tr>
<tr><td>Weather:</td><td colspan="2">Temperature:</td></tr>
<tr><td>Name of Bird:</td><td colspan="2">Type of Bird:</td></tr>
<tr><td>Type of Tail?

☐ Short
☐ Wide
☐ Fluffy
☐ Thin
☐ Long</td><td>Shape of Beak?

☐ Long & thin
☐ Short and pointed
☐ Flat and wide
☐ Hooked
☐ Cone</td><td>Birds Location?

☐ Tree
☐ Bush
☐ Feeder
☐ Fence
☐ Ground</td></tr>
<tr><td colspan="3">Any colours and markings:</td></tr>
<tr><td colspan="3">Bird's actions:</td></tr>
<tr><td colspan="3">Notes:</td></tr>
<tr><td colspan="3">Sketch/drawing:</td></tr>
</table>

My Bird Watching Journal

Date:	**Time:**	
Season:	**Habitat:**	
Location:		
Weather:	**Temperature:**	
Name of Bird:	**Type of Bird:**	
Type of Tail? ☐ Short ☐ Wide ☐ Fluffy ☐ Thin ☐ Long	**Shape of Beak?** ☐ Long & thin ☐ Short and pointed ☐ Flat and wide ☐ Hooked ☐ Cone	**Birds Location?** ☐ Tree ☐ Bush ☐ Feeder ☐ Fence ☐ Ground
Any colours and markings:		
Bird's actions:		
Notes:		
Sketch/drawing:		

My Bird Watching Journal

Date:	**Time:**	
Season:	**Habitat:**	
Location:		
Weather:	**Temperature:**	
Name of Bird:	**Type of Bird:**	
Type of Tail? ☐ Short ☐ Wide ☐ Fluffy ☐ Thin ☐ Long	**Shape of Beak?** ☐ Long & thin ☐ Short and pointed ☐ Flat and wide ☐ Hooked ☐ Cone	**Birds Location?** ☐ Tree ☐ Bush ☐ Feeder ☐ Fence ☐ Ground
Any colours and markings:		
Bird's actions:		
Notes:		
Sketch/drawing:		

My Bird Watching Journal

Date:	Time:	
Season:	Habitat:	
Location:		
Weather:	Temperature:	
Name of Bird:	Type of Bird:	
Type of Tail? ☐ Short ☐ Wide ☐ Fluffy ☐ Thin ☐ Long	**Shape of Beak?** ☐ Long & thin ☐ Short and pointed ☐ Flat and wide ☐ Hooked ☐ Cone	**Birds Location?** ☐ Tree ☐ Bush ☐ Feeder ☐ Fence ☐ Ground
Any colours and markings:		
Bird's actions:		
Notes:		
Sketch/drawing:		

My Bird Watching Journal

<table>
<tr><td>Date:</td><td colspan="2">Time:</td></tr>
<tr><td>Season:</td><td colspan="2">Habitat:</td></tr>
<tr><td colspan="3">Location:</td></tr>
<tr><td>Weather:</td><td colspan="2">Temperature:</td></tr>
<tr><td>Name of Bird:</td><td colspan="2">Type of Bird:</td></tr>
<tr><td>Type of Tail?

☐ Short
☐ Wide
☐ Fluffy
☐ Thin
☐ Long</td><td>Shape of Beak?

☐ Long & thin
☐ Short and pointed
☐ Flat and wide
☐ Hooked
☐ Cone</td><td>Birds Location?

☐ Tree
☐ Bush
☐ Feeder
☐ Fence
☐ Ground</td></tr>
<tr><td colspan="3">Any colours and markings:</td></tr>
<tr><td colspan="3">Bird's actions:</td></tr>
<tr><td colspan="3">Notes:</td></tr>
<tr><td colspan="3">Sketch/drawing:</td></tr>
</table>

My Bird Watching Journal

Date:	**Time:**	
Season:	**Habitat:**	
Location:		
Weather:	**Temperature:**	
Name of Bird:	**Type of Bird:**	
Type of Tail? ☐ Short ☐ Wide ☐ Fluffy ☐ Thin ☐ Long	**Shape of Beak?** ☐ Long & thin ☐ Short and pointed ☐ Flat and wide ☐ Hooked ☐ Cone	**Birds Location?** ☐ Tree ☐ Bush ☐ Feeder ☐ Fence ☐ Ground
Any colours and markings:		
Bird's actions:		
Notes:		
Sketch/drawing:		

My Bird Watching Journal

Date:	**Time:**	
Season:	**Habitat:**	
Location:		
Weather:	**Temperature:**	
Name of Bird:	**Type of Bird:**	
Type of Tail? ☐ Short ☐ Wide ☐ Fluffy ☐ Thin ☐ Long	**Shape of Beak?** ☐ Long & thin ☐ Short and pointed ☐ Flat and wide ☐ Hooked ☐ Cone	**Birds Location?** ☐ Tree ☐ Bush ☐ Feeder ☐ Fence ☐ Ground
Any colours and markings:		
Bird's actions:		
Notes:		
Sketch/drawing:		

My Bird Watching Journal

Season:	Habitat:	
Location:		
Weather:	Temperature:	
Name of Bird:	Type of Bird:	
Type of Tail? ☐ Short ☐ Wide ☐ Fluffy ☐ Thin ☐ Long	Shape of Beak? ☐ Long & thin ☐ Short and pointed ☐ Flat and wide ☐ Hooked ☐ Cone	Birds Location? ☐ Tree ☐ Bush ☐ Feeder ☐ Fence ☐ Ground
Any colours and markings:		
Bird's actions:		
Notes:		
Sketch/drawing:		

My Bird Watching Journal

Date:	**Time:**	
Season:	**Habitat:**	
Location:		
Weather:	**Temperature:**	
Name of Bird:	**Type of Bird:**	
Type of Tail? ☐ Short ☐ Wide ☐ Fluffy ☐ Thin ☐ Long	**Shape of Beak?** ☐ Long & thin ☐ Short and pointed ☐ Flat and wide ☐ Hooked ☐ Cone	**Birds Location?** ☐ Tree ☐ Bush ☐ Feeder ☐ Fence ☐ Ground
Any colours and markings:		
Bird's actions:		
Notes:		
Sketch/drawing:		

My Bird Watching Journal

Date:	**Time:**	
Season:	**Habitat:**	
Location:		
Weather:	**Temperature:**	
Name of Bird:	**Type of Bird:**	
Type of Tail? ☐ **Short** ☐ **Wide** ☐ **Fluffy** ☐ **Thin** ☐ **Long**	**Shape of Beak?** ☐ **Long & thin** ☐ **Short and pointed** ☐ **Flat and wide** ☐ **Hooked** ☐ **Cone**	**Birds Location?** ☐ **Tree** ☐ **Bush** ☐ **Feeder** ☐ **Fence** ☐ **Ground**
Any colours and markings:		
Bird's actions:		
Notes:		
Sketch/drawing:		

My Bird Watching Journal

Date:	**Time:**	
Season:	**Habitat:**	
Location:		
Weather:	**Temperature:**	
Name of Bird:	**Type of Bird:**	
Type of Tail? ☐ **Short** ☐ **Wide** ☐ **Fluffy** ☐ **Thin** ☐ **Long**	**Shape of Beak?** ☐ **Long & thin** ☐ **Short and pointed** ☐ **Flat and wide** ☐ **Hooked** ☐ **Cone**	**Birds Location?** ☐ **Tree** ☐ **Bush** ☐ **Feeder** ☐ **Fence** ☐ **Ground**
Any colours and markings:		
Bird's actions:		
Notes:		
Sketch/drawing:		

My Bird Watching Journal

Date:	**Time:**	
Season:	**Habitat:**	
Location:		
Weather:	**Temperature:**	
Name of Bird:	**Type of Bird:**	
Type of Tail? ☐ Short ☐ Wide ☐ Fluffy ☐ Thin ☐ Long	**Shape of Beak?** ☐ Long & thin ☐ Short and pointed ☐ Flat and wide ☐ Hooked ☐ Cone	**Birds Location?** ☐ Tree ☐ Bush ☐ Feeder ☐ Fence ☐ Ground
Any colours and markings:		
Bird's actions:		
Notes:		
Sketch/drawing:		

My Bird Watching Journal

Date:	**Time:**	
Season:	**Habitat:**	
Location:		
Weather:	**Temperature:**	
Name of Bird:	**Type of Bird:**	
Type of Tail? ☐ Short ☐ Wide ☐ Fluffy ☐ Thin ☐ Long	**Shape of Beak?** ☐ Long & thin ☐ Short and pointed ☐ Flat and wide ☐ Hooked ☐ Cone	**Birds Location?** ☐ Tree ☐ Bush ☐ Feeder ☐ Fence ☐ Ground
Any colours and markings:		
Bird's actions:		
Notes:		
Sketch/drawing:		

My Bird Watching Journal

Date:	**Time:**	
Season:	**Habitat:**	
Location:		
Weather:	**Temperature:**	
Name of Bird:	**Type of Bird:**	
Type of Tail? ☐ Short ☐ Wide ☐ Fluffy ☐ Thin ☐ Long	**Shape of Beak?** ☐ Long & thin ☐ Short and pointed ☐ Flat and wide ☐ Hooked ☐ Cone	**Birds Location?** ☐ Tree ☐ Bush ☐ Feeder ☐ Fence ☐ Ground
Any colours and markings:		
Bird's actions:		
Notes:		
Sketch/drawing:		

My Bird Watching Journal

Date:	**Time:**	
Season:	**Habitat:**	
Location:		
Weather:	**Temperature:**	
Name of Bird:	**Type of Bird:**	
Type of Tail? ☐ **Short** ☐ **Wide** ☐ **Fluffy** ☐ **Thin** ☐ **Long**	**Shape of Beak?** ☐ **Long & thin** ☐ **Short and pointed** ☐ **Flat and wide** ☐ **Hooked** ☐ **Cone**	**Birds Location?** ☐ **Tree** ☐ **Bush** ☐ **Feeder** ☐ **Fence** ☐ **Ground**
Any colours and markings:		
Bird's actions:		
Notes:		
Sketch/drawing:		

My Bird Watching Journal

Date:	**Time:**	
Season:	**Habitat:**	
Location:		
Weather:	**Temperature:**	
Name of Bird:	**Type of Bird:**	
Type of Tail? ☐ **Short** ☐ **Wide** ☐ **Fluffy** ☐ **Thin** ☐ **Long**	**Shape of Beak?** ☐ **Long & thin** ☐ **Short and pointed** ☐ **Flat and wide** ☐ **Hooked** ☐ **Cone**	**Birds Location?** ☐ **Tree** ☐ **Bush** ☐ **Feeder** ☐ **Fence** ☐ **Ground**
Any colours and markings:		
Bird's actions:		
Notes:		
Sketch/drawing:		

My Bird Watching Journal

Date:	Time:	
Season:	**Habitat:**	
Location:		
Weather:	**Temperature:**	
Name of Bird:	**Type of Bird:**	
Type of Tail? ☐ Short ☐ Wide ☐ Fluffy ☐ Thin ☐ Long	**Shape of Beak?** ☐ Long & thin ☐ Short and pointed ☐ Flat and wide ☐ Hooked ☐ Cone	**Birds Location?** ☐ Tree ☐ Bush ☐ Feeder ☐ Fence ☐ Ground
Any colours and markings:		
Bird's actions:		
Notes:		
Sketch/drawing:		

My Bird Watching Journal

Season:	**Habitat:**	
Location:		
Weather:	**Temperature:**	
Name of Bird:	**Type of Bird:**	
Type of Tail? ☐ Short ☐ Wide ☐ Fluffy ☐ Thin ☐ Long	**Shape of Beak?** ☐ Long & thin ☐ Short and pointed ☐ Flat and wide ☐ Hooked ☐ Cone	**Birds Location?** ☐ Tree ☐ Bush ☐ Feeder ☐ Fence ☐ Ground
Any colours and markings:		
Bird's actions:		
Notes:		
Sketch/drawing:		

My Bird Watching Journal

Date:	Time:	
Season:	Habitat:	
Location:		
Weather:	Temperature:	
Name of Bird:	Type of Bird:	
Type of Tail?	Shape of Beak?	Birds Location?
☐ Short ☐ Wide ☐ Fluffy ☐ Thin ☐ Long	☐ Long & thin ☐ Short and pointed ☐ Flat and wide ☐ Hooked ☐ Cone	☐ Tree ☐ Bush ☐ Feeder ☐ Fence ☐ Ground
Any colours and markings:		
Bird's actions:		
Notes:		
Sketch/drawing:		

My Bird Watching Journal

Date:	**Time:**	
Season:	**Habitat:**	
Location:		
Weather:	**Temperature:**	
Name of Bird:	**Type of Bird:**	
Type of Tail? ☐ Short ☐ Wide ☐ Fluffy ☐ Thin ☐ Long	**Shape of Beak?** ☐ Long & thin ☐ Short and pointed ☐ Flat and wide ☐ Hooked ☐ Cone	**Birds Location?** ☐ Tree ☐ Bush ☐ Feeder ☐ Fence ☐ Ground
Any colours and markings:		
Bird's actions:		
Notes:		
Sketch/drawing:		

My Bird Watching Journal

Date:	**Time:**	
Season:	**Habitat:**	
Location:		
Weather:	**Temperature:**	
Name of Bird:	**Type of Bird:**	
Type of Tail? ☐ Short ☐ Wide ☐ Fluffy ☐ Thin ☐ Long	**Shape of Beak?** ☐ Long & thin ☐ Short and pointed ☐ Flat and wide ☐ Hooked ☐ Cone	**Birds Location?** ☐ Tree ☐ Bush ☐ Feeder ☐ Fence ☐ Ground
Any colours and markings:		
Bird's actions:		
Notes:		
Sketch/drawing:		

My Bird Watching Journal

Date:	**Time:**	
Season:	**Habitat:**	
Location:		
Weather:	**Temperature:**	
Name of Bird:	**Type of Bird:**	
Type of Tail?	**Shape of Beak?**	**Birds Location?**
☐ **Short**	☐ **Long & thin**	☐ **Tree**
☐ **Wide**	☐ **Short and pointed**	☐ **Bush**
☐ **Fluffy**	☐ **Flat and wide**	☐ **Feeder**
☐ **Thin**	☐ **Hooked**	☐ **Fence**
☐ **Long**	☐ **Cone**	☐ **Ground**
Any colours and markings:		
Bird's actions:		
Notes:		
Sketch/drawing:		

My Bird Watching Journal

Season:	**Habitat:**	
Location:		
Weather:	**Temperature:**	
Name of Bird:	**Type of Bird:**	
Type of Tail? ☐ Short ☐ Wide ☐ Fluffy ☐ Thin ☐ Long	**Shape of Beak?** ☐ Long & thin ☐ Short and pointed ☐ Flat and wide ☐ Hooked ☐ Cone	**Birds Location?** ☐ Tree ☐ Bush ☐ Feeder ☐ Fence ☐ Ground
Any colours and markings:		
Bird's actions:		
Notes:		
Sketch/drawing:		
Date:	**Time:**	

My Bird Watching Journal

Season:	Habitat:	
Location:		
Weather:	Temperature:	
Name of Bird:	Type of Bird:	
Type of Tail? ☐ Short ☐ Wide ☐ Fluffy ☐ Thin ☐ Long	Shape of Beak? ☐ Long & thin ☐ Short and pointed ☐ Flat and wide ☐ Hooked ☐ Cone	Birds Location? ☐ Tree ☐ Bush ☐ Feeder ☐ Fence ☐ Ground
Any colours and markings:		
Bird's actions:		
Notes:		
Sketch/drawing:		
Date:	Time:	

My Bird Watching Journal

Season:	**Habitat:**	
Location:		
Weather:	**Temperature:**	
Name of Bird:	**Type of Bird:**	
Type of Tail? ☐ Short ☐ Wide ☐ Fluffy ☐ Thin ☐ Long	**Shape of Beak?** ☐ Long & thin ☐ Short and pointed ☐ Flat and wide ☐ Hooked ☐ Cone	**Birds Location?** ☐ Tree ☐ Bush ☐ Feeder ☐ Fence ☐ Ground
Any colours and markings:		
Bird's actions:		
Notes:		
Sketch/drawing:		
Date:	**Time:**	

My Bird Watching Journal

Season:	**Habitat:**	
Location:		
Weather:	**Temperature:**	
Name of Bird:	**Type of Bird:**	
Type of Tail? ☐ Short ☐ Wide ☐ Fluffy ☐ Thin ☐ Long	**Shape of Beak?** ☐ Long & thin ☐ Short and pointed ☐ Flat and wide ☐ Hooked ☐ Cone	**Birds Location?** ☐ Tree ☐ Bush ☐ Feeder ☐ Fence ☐ Ground
Any colours and markings:		
Bird's actions:		
Notes:		
Sketch/drawing:		

My Bird Watching Journal

Date:	**Time:**	
Season:	**Habitat:**	
Location:		
Weather:	**Temperature:**	
Name of Bird:	**Type of Bird:**	
Type of Tail? ☐ Short ☐ Wide ☐ Fluffy ☐ Thin ☐ Long	**Shape of Beak?** ☐ Long & thin ☐ Short and pointed ☐ Flat and wide ☐ Hooked ☐ Cone	**Birds Location?** ☐ Tree ☐ Bush ☐ Feeder ☐ Fence ☐ Ground
Any colours and markings:		
Bird's actions:		
Notes:		
Sketch/drawing:		

My Bird Watching Journal

Season:	Habitat:	
Location:		
Weather:	Temperature:	
Name of Bird:	Type of Bird:	
Type of Tail? ☐ Short ☐ Wide ☐ Fluffy ☐ Thin ☐ Long	Shape of Beak? ☐ Long & thin ☐ Short and pointed ☐ Flat and wide ☐ Hooked ☐ Cone	Birds Location? ☐ Tree ☐ Bush ☐ Feeder ☐ Fence ☐ Ground
Any colours and markings:		
Bird's actions:		
Notes:		
Sketch/drawing:		

My Bird Watching Journal

Date:	**Time:**	
Season:	**Habitat:**	
Location:		
Weather:	**Temperature:**	
Name of Bird:	**Type of Bird:**	
Type of Tail? ☐ **Short** ☐ **Wide** ☐ **Fluffy** ☐ **Thin** ☐ **Long**	**Shape of Beak?** ☐ **Long & thin** ☐ **Short and pointed** ☐ **Flat and wide** ☐ **Hooked** ☐ **Cone**	**Birds Location?** ☐ **Tree** ☐ **Bush** ☐ **Feeder** ☐ **Fence** ☐ **Ground**
Any colours and markings:		
Bird's actions:		
Notes:		
Sketch/drawing:		

My Bird Watching Journal

Date:	Time:	
Season:	Habitat:	
Location:		
Weather:	Temperature:	
Name of Bird:	Type of Bird:	
Type of Tail? ☐ Short ☐ Wide ☐ Fluffy ☐ Thin ☐ Long	Shape of Beak? ☐ Long & thin ☐ Short and pointed ☐ Flat and wide ☐ Hooked ☐ Cone	Birds Location? ☐ Tree ☐ Bush ☐ Feeder ☐ Fence ☐ Ground
Any colours and markings:		
Bird's actions:		
Notes:		
Sketch/drawing:		

My Bird Watching Journal

Date:	**Time:**	
Season:	**Habitat:**	
Location:		
Weather:	**Temperature:**	
Name of Bird:	**Type of Bird:**	
Type of Tail? ☐ Short ☐ Wide ☐ Fluffy ☐ Thin ☐ Long	**Shape of Beak?** ☐ Long & thin ☐ Short and pointed ☐ Flat and wide ☐ Hooked ☐ Cone	**Birds Location?** ☐ Tree ☐ Bush ☐ Feeder ☐ Fence ☐ Ground
Any colours and markings:		
Bird's actions:		
Notes:		
Sketch/drawing:		

My Bird Watching Journal

Date:	**Time:**	
Season:	**Habitat:**	
Location:		
Weather:	**Temperature:**	
Name of Bird:	**Type of Bird:**	
Type of Tail? ☐ Short ☐ Wide ☐ Fluffy ☐ Thin ☐ Long	**Shape of Beak?** ☐ Long & thin ☐ Short and pointed ☐ Flat and wide ☐ Hooked ☐ Cone	**Birds Location?** ☐ Tree ☐ Bush ☐ Feeder ☐ Fence ☐ Ground
Any colours and markings:		
Bird's actions:		
Notes:		
Sketch/drawing:		

My Bird Watching Journal

Date:	**Time:**	
Season:	**Habitat:**	
Location:		
Weather:	**Temperature:**	
Name of Bird:	**Type of Bird:**	
Type of Tail? ☐ Short ☐ Wide ☐ Fluffy ☐ Thin ☐ Long	**Shape of Beak?** ☐ Long & thin ☐ Short and pointed ☐ Flat and wide ☐ Hooked ☐ Cone	**Birds Location?** ☐ Tree ☐ Bush ☐ Feeder ☐ Fence ☐ Ground
Any colours and markings:		
Bird's actions:		
Notes:		
Sketch/drawing:		

My Bird Watching Journal

Date:	Time:	
Season:	Habitat:	
Location:		
Weather:	Temperature:	
Name of Bird:	Type of Bird:	
Type of Tail? ☐ Short ☐ Wide ☐ Fluffy ☐ Thin ☐ Long	Shape of Beak? ☐ Long & thin ☐ Short and pointed ☐ Flat and wide ☐ Hooked ☐ Cone	Birds Location? ☐ Tree ☐ Bush ☐ Feeder ☐ Fence ☐ Ground
Any colours and markings:		
Bird's actions:		
Notes:		
Sketch/drawing:		

My Bird Watching Journal

Date:	**Time:**	
Season:	**Habitat:**	
Location:		
Weather:	**Temperature:**	
Name of Bird:	**Type of Bird:**	
Type of Tail? ☐ Short ☐ Wide ☐ Fluffy ☐ Thin ☐ Long	**Shape of Beak?** ☐ Long & thin ☐ Short and pointed ☐ Flat and wide ☐ Hooked ☐ Cone	**Birds Location?** ☐ Tree ☐ Bush ☐ Feeder ☐ Fence ☐ Ground
Any colours and markings:		
Bird's actions:		
Notes:		
Sketch/drawing:		

My Bird Watching Journal

Date:	**Time:**	
Season:	**Habitat:**	
Location:		
Weather:	**Temperature:**	
Name of Bird:	**Type of Bird:**	
Type of Tail? ☐ **Short** ☐ **Wide** ☐ **Fluffy** ☐ **Thin** ☐ **Long**	**Shape of Beak?** ☐ **Long & thin** ☐ **Short and pointed** ☐ **Flat and wide** ☐ **Hooked** ☐ **Cone**	**Birds Location?** ☐ **Tree** ☐ **Bush** ☐ **Feeder** ☐ **Fence** ☐ **Ground**
Any colours and markings:		
Bird's actions:		
Notes:		
Sketch/drawing:		

My Bird Watching Journal

Date:	Time:	
Season:	Habitat:	
Location:		
Weather:	Temperature:	
Name of Bird:	Type of Bird:	
Type of Tail? ☐ Short ☐ Wide ☐ Fluffy ☐ Thin ☐ Long	Shape of Beak? ☐ Long & thin ☐ Short and pointed ☐ Flat and wide ☐ Hooked ☐ Cone	Birds Location? ☐ Tree ☐ Bush ☐ Feeder ☐ Fence ☐ Ground
Any colours and markings:		
Bird's actions:		
Notes:		
Sketch/drawing:		

My Bird Watching Journal

<table>
<tr><td>Season:</td><td colspan="2">Habitat:</td></tr>
<tr><td colspan="3">Location:</td></tr>
<tr><td>Weather:</td><td colspan="2">Temperature:</td></tr>
<tr><td>Name of Bird:</td><td colspan="2">Type of Bird:</td></tr>
<tr><td>Type of Tail?

☐ Short
☐ Wide
☐ Fluffy
☐ Thin
☐ Long</td><td>Shape of Beak?

☐ Long & thin
☐ Short and pointed
☐ Flat and wide
☐ Hooked
☐ Cone</td><td>Birds Location?

☐ Tree
☐ Bush
☐ Feeder
☐ Fence
☐ Ground</td></tr>
<tr><td colspan="3">Any colours and markings:</td></tr>
<tr><td colspan="3">Bird's actions:</td></tr>
<tr><td colspan="3">Notes:</td></tr>
<tr><td colspan="3">Sketch/drawing:</td></tr>
</table>

My Bird Watching Journal

Date:	**Time:**	
Season:	**Habitat:**	
Location:		
Weather:	**Temperature:**	
Name of Bird:	**Type of Bird:**	
Type of Tail? ☐ Short ☐ Wide ☐ Fluffy ☐ Thin ☐ Long	**Shape of Beak?** ☐ Long & thin ☐ Short and pointed ☐ Flat and wide ☐ Hooked ☐ Cone	**Birds Location?** ☐ Tree ☐ Bush ☐ Feeder ☐ Fence ☐ Ground
Any colours and markings:		
Bird's actions:		
Notes:		
Sketch/drawing:		

My Bird Watching Journal

Date:	**Time:**	
Season:	**Habitat:**	
Location:		
Weather:	**Temperature:**	
Name of Bird:	**Type of Bird:**	
Type of Tail? ☐ Short ☐ Wide ☐ Fluffy ☐ Thin ☐ Long	**Shape of Beak?** ☐ Long & thin ☐ Short and pointed ☐ Flat and wide ☐ Hooked ☐ Cone	**Birds Location?** ☐ Tree ☐ Bush ☐ Feeder ☐ Fence ☐ Ground
Any colours and markings:		
Bird's actions:		
Notes:		
Sketch/drawing:		

My Bird Watching Journal

Date:	**Time:**	
Season:	**Habitat:**	
Location:		
Weather:	**Temperature:**	
Name of Bird:	**Type of Bird:**	
Type of Tail? ☐ Short ☐ Wide ☐ Fluffy ☐ Thin ☐ Long	**Shape of Beak?** ☐ Long & thin ☐ Short and pointed ☐ Flat and wide ☐ Hooked ☐ Cone	**Birds Location?** ☐ Tree ☐ Bush ☐ Feeder ☐ Fence ☐ Ground
Any colours and markings:		
Bird's actions:		
Notes:		
Sketch/drawing:		

My Bird Watching Journal

Date:

Time:

Date: **Time:**

Season:

Habitat:

Location:

Weather:

Temperature:

Name of Bird:

Type of Bird:

Type of Tail?

- ☐ Short
- ☐ Wide
- ☐ Fluffy
- ☐ Thin
- ☐ Long

Shape of Beak?

- ☐ Long & thin
- ☐ Short and pointed
- ☐ Flat and wide
- ☐ Hooked
- ☐ Cone

Birds Location?

- ☐ Tree
- ☐ Bush
- ☐ Feeder
- ☐ Fence
- ☐ Ground

Any colours and markings:

Bird's actions:

Notes:

Sketch/drawing:

My Bird Watching Journal

Season:	Habitat:	
Location:		
Weather:	Temperature:	
Name of Bird:	Type of Bird:	
Type of Tail? ☐ Short ☐ Wide ☐ Fluffy ☐ Thin ☐ Long	Shape of Beak? ☐ Long & thin ☐ Short and pointed ☐ Flat and wide ☐ Hooked ☐ Cone	Birds Location? ☐ Tree ☐ Bush ☐ Feeder ☐ Fence ☐ Ground
Any colours and markings:		
Bird's actions:		
Notes:		
Sketch/drawing:		
Date:	Time:	

My Bird Watching Journal

Season:	**Habitat:**	
Location:		
Weather:	**Temperature:**	
Name of Bird:	**Type of Bird:**	
Type of Tail? ☐ Short ☐ Wide ☐ Fluffy ☐ Thin ☐ Long	**Shape of Beak?** ☐ Long & thin ☐ Short and pointed ☐ Flat and wide ☐ Hooked ☐ Cone	**Birds Location?** ☐ Tree ☐ Bush ☐ Feeder ☐ Fence ☐ Ground
Any colours and markings:		
Bird's actions:		
Notes:		
Sketch/drawing:		
Date:	**Time:**	

My Bird Watching Journal

Season:	Habitat:	
Location:		
Weather:	Temperature:	
Name of Bird:	Type of Bird:	
Type of Tail? ☐ Short ☐ Wide ☐ Fluffy ☐ Thin ☐ Long	**Shape of Beak?** ☐ Long & thin ☐ Short and pointed ☐ Flat and wide ☐ Hooked ☐ Cone	**Birds Location?** ☐ Tree ☐ Bush ☐ Feeder ☐ Fence ☐ Ground
Any colours and markings:		
Bird's actions:		
Notes:		
Sketch/drawing:		
Date:	Time:	

My Bird Watching Journal

Season:	Habitat:	
Location:		
Weather:	Temperature:	
Name of Bird:	Type of Bird:	
Type of Tail? ☐ Short ☐ Wide ☐ Fluffy ☐ Thin ☐ Long	Shape of Beak? ☐ Long & thin ☐ Short and pointed ☐ Flat and wide ☐ Hooked ☐ Cone	Birds Location? ☐ Tree ☐ Bush ☐ Feeder ☐ Fence ☐ Ground
Any colours and markings:		
Bird's actions:		
Notes:		
Sketch/drawing:		

My Bird Watching Journal

Date:	**Time:**	
Season:	**Habitat:**	
Location:		
Weather:	**Temperature:**	
Name of Bird:	**Type of Bird:**	
Type of Tail?	**Shape of Beak?**	**Birds Location?**
☐ Short	☐ Long & thin	☐ Tree
☐ Wide	☐ Short and pointed	☐ Bush
☐ Fluffy	☐ Flat and wide	☐ Feeder
☐ Thin	☐ Hooked	☐ Fence
☐ Long	☐ Cone	☐ Ground
Any colours and markings:		
Bird's actions:		
Notes:		
Sketch/drawing:		

My Bird Watching Journal

Season:	**Habitat:**	
Location:		
Weather:	**Temperature:**	
Name of Bird:	**Type of Bird:**	
Type of Tail? ☐ Short ☐ Wide ☐ Fluffy ☐ Thin ☐ Long	**Shape of Beak?** ☐ Long & thin ☐ Short and pointed ☐ Flat and wide ☐ Hooked ☐ Cone	**Birds Location?** ☐ Tree ☐ Bush ☐ Feeder ☐ Fence ☐ Ground
Any colours and markings:		
Bird's actions:		
Notes:		
Sketch/drawing:		

My Bird Watching Journal

Date:	**Time:**	
Season:	**Habitat:**	
Location:		
Weather:	**Temperature:**	
Name of Bird:	**Type of Bird:**	
Type of Tail? ☐ Short ☐ Wide ☐ Fluffy ☐ Thin ☐ Long	**Shape of Beak?** ☐ Long & thin ☐ Short and pointed ☐ Flat and wide ☐ Hooked ☐ Cone	**Birds Location?** ☐ Tree ☐ Bush ☐ Feeder ☐ Fence ☐ Ground
Any colours and markings:		
Bird's actions:		
Notes:		
Sketch/drawing:		

My Bird Watching Journal

Date:	**Time:**	
Season:	**Habitat:**	
Location:		
Weather:	**Temperature:**	
Name of Bird:	**Type of Bird:**	
Type of Tail? ☐ Short ☐ Wide ☐ Fluffy ☐ Thin ☐ Long	**Shape of Beak?** ☐ Long & thin ☐ Short and pointed ☐ Flat and wide ☐ Hooked ☐ Cone	**Birds Location?** ☐ Tree ☐ Bush ☐ Feeder ☐ Fence ☐ Ground
Any colours and markings:		
Bird's actions:		
Notes:		
Sketch/drawing:		

My Bird Watching Journal

<table>
<tr><td>Date:</td><td colspan="2">Time:</td></tr>
<tr><td>Season:</td><td colspan="2">Habitat:</td></tr>
<tr><td colspan="3">Location:</td></tr>
<tr><td>Weather:</td><td colspan="2">Temperature:</td></tr>
<tr><td>Name of Bird:</td><td colspan="2">Type of Bird:</td></tr>
<tr><td>Type of Tail?

☐ Short
☐ Wide
☐ Fluffy
☐ Thin
☐ Long</td><td>Shape of Beak?

☐ Long & thin
☐ Short and pointed
☐ Flat and wide
☐ Hooked
☐ Cone</td><td>Birds Location?

☐ Tree
☐ Bush
☐ Feeder
☐ Fence
☐ Ground</td></tr>
<tr><td colspan="3">Any colours and markings:</td></tr>
<tr><td colspan="3">Bird's actions:</td></tr>
<tr><td colspan="3">Notes:</td></tr>
<tr><td colspan="3">Sketch/drawing:</td></tr>
</table>

My Bird Watching Journal

Date:	**Time:**	
Season:	**Habitat:**	
Location:		
Weather:	**Temperature:**	
Name of Bird:	**Type of Bird:**	
Type of Tail? ☐ Short ☐ Wide ☐ Fluffy ☐ Thin ☐ Long	**Shape of Beak?** ☐ Long & thin ☐ Short and pointed ☐ Flat and wide ☐ Hooked ☐ Cone	**Birds Location?** ☐ Tree ☐ Bush ☐ Feeder ☐ Fence ☐ Ground
Any colours and markings:		
Bird's actions:		
Notes:		
Sketch/drawing:		

My Bird Watching Journal

Date:	**Time:**	
Season:	**Habitat:**	
Location:		
Weather:	**Temperature:**	
Name of Bird:	**Type of Bird:**	
Type of Tail? ☐ Short ☐ Wide ☐ Fluffy ☐ Thin ☐ Long	**Shape of Beak?** ☐ Long & thin ☐ Short and pointed ☐ Flat and wide ☐ Hooked ☐ Cone	**Birds Location?** ☐ Tree ☐ Bush ☐ Feeder ☐ Fence ☐ Ground
Any colours and markings:		
Bird's actions:		
Notes:		
Sketch/drawing:		

My Bird Watching Journal

Date:	**Time:**	
Season:	**Habitat:**	
Location:		
Weather:	**Temperature:**	
Name of Bird:	**Type of Bird:**	
Type of Tail? ☐ Short ☐ Wide ☐ Fluffy ☐ Thin ☐ Long	**Shape of Beak?** ☐ Long & thin ☐ Short and pointed ☐ Flat and wide ☐ Hooked ☐ Cone	**Birds Location?** ☐ Tree ☐ Bush ☐ Feeder ☐ Fence ☐ Ground
Any colours and markings:		
Bird's actions:		
Notes:		
Sketch/drawing:		

My Bird Watching Journal

Date:	**Time:**	
Season:	**Habitat:**	
Location:		
Weather:	**Temperature:**	
Name of Bird:	**Type of Bird:**	
Type of Tail? ☐ Short ☐ Wide ☐ Fluffy ☐ Thin ☐ Long	**Shape of Beak?** ☐ Long & thin ☐ Short and pointed ☐ Flat and wide ☐ Hooked ☐ Cone	**Birds Location?** ☐ Tree ☐ Bush ☐ Feeder ☐ Fence ☐ Ground
Any colours and markings:		
Bird's actions:		
Notes:		
Sketch/drawing:		

My Bird Watching Journal

Date:	**Time:**	
Season:	**Habitat:**	
Location:		
Weather:	**Temperature:**	
Name of Bird:	**Type of Bird:**	
Type of Tail? ☐ Short ☐ Wide ☐ Fluffy ☐ Thin ☐ Long	**Shape of Beak?** ☐ Long & thin ☐ Short and pointed ☐ Flat and wide ☐ Hooked ☐ Cone	**Birds Location?** ☐ Tree ☐ Bush ☐ Feeder ☐ Fence ☐ Ground
Any colours and markings:		
Bird's actions:		
Notes:		
Sketch/drawing:		

My Bird Watching Journal

Date:	**Time:**	
Season:	**Habitat:**	
Location:		
Weather:	**Temperature:**	
Name of Bird:	**Type of Bird:**	
Type of Tail? ☐ Short ☐ Wide ☐ Fluffy ☐ Thin ☐ Long	**Shape of Beak?** ☐ Long & thin ☐ Short and pointed ☐ Flat and wide ☐ Hooked ☐ Cone	**Birds Location?** ☐ Tree ☐ Bush ☐ Feeder ☐ Fence ☐ Ground
Any colours and markings:		
Bird's actions:		
Notes:		
Sketch/drawing:		

My Bird Watching Journal

Season:	Habitat:	
Location:		
Weather:	Temperature:	
Name of Bird:	Type of Bird:	
Type of Tail? ☐ Short ☐ Wide ☐ Fluffy ☐ Thin ☐ Long	Shape of Beak? ☐ Long & thin ☐ Short and pointed ☐ Flat and wide ☐ Hooked ☐ Cone	Birds Location? ☐ Tree ☐ Bush ☐ Feeder ☐ Fence ☐ Ground
Any colours and markings:		
Bird's actions:		
Notes:		
Sketch/drawing:		

My Bird Watching Journal

Date:	**Time:**	
Season:	**Habitat:**	
Location:		
Weather:	**Temperature:**	
Name of Bird:	**Type of Bird:**	
Type of Tail? ☐ Short ☐ Wide ☐ Fluffy ☐ Thin ☐ Long	**Shape of Beak?** ☐ Long & thin ☐ Short and pointed ☐ Flat and wide ☐ Hooked ☐ Cone	**Birds Location?** ☐ Tree ☐ Bush ☐ Feeder ☐ Fence ☐ Ground
Any colours and markings:		
Bird's actions:		
Notes:		
Sketch/drawing:		

My Bird Watching Journal

Date:	**Time:**	
Season:	**Habitat:**	
Location:		
Weather:	**Temperature:**	
Name of Bird:	**Type of Bird:**	
Type of Tail? ☐ Short ☐ Wide ☐ Fluffy ☐ Thin ☐ Long	**Shape of Beak?** ☐ Long & thin ☐ Short and pointed ☐ Flat and wide ☐ Hooked ☐ Cone	**Birds Location?** ☐ Tree ☐ Bush ☐ Feeder ☐ Fence ☐ Ground
Any colours and markings:		
Bird's actions:		
Notes:		
Sketch/drawing:		

My Bird Watching Journal

Date:	Time:	
Season:	Habitat:	
Location:		
Weather:	Temperature:	
Name of Bird:	Type of Bird:	
Type of Tail? ☐ Short ☐ Wide ☐ Fluffy ☐ Thin ☐ Long	Shape of Beak? ☐ Long & thin ☐ Short and pointed ☐ Flat and wide ☐ Hooked ☐ Cone	Birds Location? ☐ Tree ☐ Bush ☐ Feeder ☐ Fence ☐ Ground
Any colours and markings:		
Bird's actions:		
Notes:		
Sketch/drawing:		

My Bird Watching Journal

Date:	**Time:**	
Season:	**Habitat:**	
Location:		
Weather:	**Temperature:**	
Name of Bird:	**Type of Bird:**	
Type of Tail? ☐ Short ☐ Wide ☐ Fluffy ☐ Thin ☐ Long	**Shape of Beak?** ☐ Long & thin ☐ Short and pointed ☐ Flat and wide ☐ Hooked ☐ Cone	**Birds Location?** ☐ Tree ☐ Bush ☐ Feeder ☐ Fence ☐ Ground
Any colours and markings:		
Bird's actions:		
Notes:		
Sketch/drawing:		

My Bird Watching Journal

Date:	**Time:**	
Season:	**Habitat:**	
Location:		
Weather:	**Temperature:**	
Name of Bird:	**Type of Bird:**	
Type of Tail? ☐ Short ☐ Wide ☐ Fluffy ☐ Thin ☐ Long	**Shape of Beak?** ☐ Long & thin ☐ Short and pointed ☐ Flat and wide ☐ Hooked ☐ Cone	**Birds Location?** ☐ Tree ☐ Bush ☐ Feeder ☐ Fence ☐ Ground
Any colours and markings:		
Bird's actions:		
Notes:		
Sketch/drawing:		

My Bird Watching Journal

Date:	Time:	
Season:	Habitat:	
Location:		
Weather:	Temperature:	
Name of Bird:	Type of Bird:	
Type of Tail? ☐ Short ☐ Wide ☐ Fluffy ☐ Thin ☐ Long	Shape of Beak? ☐ Long & thin ☐ Short and pointed ☐ Flat and wide ☐ Hooked ☐ Cone	Birds Location? ☐ Tree ☐ Bush ☐ Feeder ☐ Fence ☐ Ground
Any colours and markings:		
Bird's actions:		
Notes:		
Sketch/drawing:		

My Bird Watching Journal

Date:	**Time:**	
Season:	**Habitat:**	
Location:		
Weather:	**Temperature:**	
Name of Bird:	**Type of Bird:**	
Type of Tail? ☐ Short ☐ Wide ☐ Fluffy ☐ Thin ☐ Long	**Shape of Beak?** ☐ Long & thin ☐ Short and pointed ☐ Flat and wide ☐ Hooked ☐ Cone	**Birds Location?** ☐ Tree ☐ Bush ☐ Feeder ☐ Fence ☐ Ground
Any colours and markings:		
Bird's actions:		
Notes:		
Sketch/drawing:		

My Bird Watching Journal

Date:	**Time:**	
Season:	**Habitat:**	
Location:		
Weather:	**Temperature:**	
Name of Bird:	**Type of Bird:**	
Type of Tail? ☐ Short ☐ Wide ☐ Fluffy ☐ Thin ☐ Long	**Shape of Beak?** ☐ Long & thin ☐ Short and pointed ☐ Flat and wide ☐ Hooked ☐ Cone	**Birds Location?** ☐ Tree ☐ Bush ☐ Feeder ☐ Fence ☐ Ground
Any colours and markings:		
Bird's actions:		
Notes:		
Sketch/drawing:		

My Bird Watching Journal

Date:	Time:	
Season:	Habitat:	
Location:		
Weather:	Temperature:	
Name of Bird:	Type of Bird:	
Type of Tail? ☐ Short ☐ Wide ☐ Fluffy ☐ Thin ☐ Long	Shape of Beak? ☐ Long & thin ☐ Short and pointed ☐ Flat and wide ☐ Hooked ☐ Cone	Birds Location? ☐ Tree ☐ Bush ☐ Feeder ☐ Fence ☐ Ground
Any colours and markings:		
Bird's actions:		
Notes:		
Sketch/drawing:		

My Bird Watching Journal

Season:	**Habitat:**	
Location:		
Weather:	**Temperature:**	
Name of Bird:	**Type of Bird:**	
Type of Tail? ☐ Short ☐ Wide ☐ Fluffy ☐ Thin ☐ Long	**Shape of Beak?** ☐ Long & thin ☐ Short and pointed ☐ Flat and wide ☐ Hooked ☐ Cone	**Birds Location?** ☐ Tree ☐ Bush ☐ Feeder ☐ Fence ☐ Ground
Any colours and markings:		
Bird's actions:		
Notes:		
Sketch/drawing:		

My Bird Watching Journal

Date:	**Time:**	
Season:	**Habitat:**	
Location:		
Weather:	**Temperature:**	
Name of Bird:	**Type of Bird:**	
Type of Tail? ☐ Short ☐ Wide ☐ Fluffy ☐ Thin ☐ Long	**Shape of Beak?** ☐ Long & thin ☐ Short and pointed ☐ Flat and wide ☐ Hooked ☐ Cone	**Birds Location?** ☐ Tree ☐ Bush ☐ Feeder ☐ Fence ☐ Ground
Any colours and markings:		
Bird's actions:		
Notes:		
Sketch/drawing:		

My Bird Watching Journal

Date:	**Time:**	
Season:	**Habitat:**	
Location:		
Weather:	**Temperature:**	
Name of Bird:	**Type of Bird:**	
Type of Tail? ☐ Short ☐ Wide ☐ Fluffy ☐ Thin ☐ Long	**Shape of Beak?** ☐ Long & thin ☐ Short and pointed ☐ Flat and wide ☐ Hooked ☐ Cone	**Birds Location?** ☐ Tree ☐ Bush ☐ Feeder ☐ Fence ☐ Ground
Any colours and markings:		
Bird's actions:		
Notes:		
Sketch/drawing:		

My Bird Watching Journal

Date:	**Time:**	
Season:	**Habitat:**	
Location:		
Weather:	**Temperature:**	
Name of Bird:	**Type of Bird:**	
Type of Tail? ☐ Short ☐ Wide ☐ Fluffy ☐ Thin ☐ Long	**Shape of Beak?** ☐ Long & thin ☐ Short and pointed ☐ Flat and wide ☐ Hooked ☐ Cone	**Birds Location?** ☐ Tree ☐ Bush ☐ Feeder ☐ Fence ☐ Ground
Any colours and markings:		
Bird's actions:		
Notes:		
Sketch/drawing:		

My Bird Watching Journal

Date:	**Time:**
Season:	**Habitat:**
Location:	
Weather:	**Temperature:**
Name of Bird:	**Type of Bird:**

Type of Tail?	**Shape of Beak?**	**Birds Location?**
☐ **Short**	☐ **Long & thin**	☐ **Tree**
☐ **Wide**	☐ **Short and pointed**	☐ **Bush**
☐ **Fluffy**	☐ **Flat and wide**	☐ **Feeder**
☐ **Thin**	☐ **Hooked**	☐ **Fence**
☐ **Long**	☐ **Cone**	☐ **Ground**

Any colours and markings:
Bird's actions:
Notes:
Sketch/drawing:

My Bird Watching Journal

Date:	Time:	
Season:	Habitat:	
Location:		
Weather:	Temperature:	
Name of Bird:	Type of Bird:	
Type of Tail? ☐ Short ☐ Wide ☐ Fluffy ☐ Thin ☐ Long	Shape of Beak? ☐ Long & thin ☐ Short and pointed ☐ Flat and wide ☐ Hooked ☐ Cone	Birds Location? ☐ Tree ☐ Bush ☐ Feeder ☐ Fence ☐ Ground
Any colours and markings:		
Bird's actions:		
Notes:		
Sketch/drawing:		

My Bird Watching Journal